DRIVING STANDARDS AGENCY

C000076549

DRIVING SKILLS

THE OFFICIAL DSA GUIDE TO
COMPULSORY BASIC TRAINING
for Motorcyclists

London: The Stationery Office

Published by The Stationery Office

© Crown Copyright 1998

Applications for reproduction should be made in writing to
The Copyright Unit, Her Majesty's Stationery Office,
St Clements House, 2–16 Colegate, Norwich NR3 1BQ

ISBN 0 11 552013 9

A CIP catalogue record for this book is available from the
British Library

Other titles in the Driving Skills series

The Official Theory Test for Car Drivers and Motorcyclists

The Official Theory Test for Drivers of Large Vehicles

The Driving Test

The Driving Manual

The Bus and Coach Driving Manual

The Goods Vehicle Driving Manual

The Motorcycling Manual

The Theory Test and Beyond (CD-ROM)

Acknowledgments

The Driving Standards Agency (DSA) would like to thank the staff of the
following organisations for their contribution to the production of this
publication

Department of the Environment, Transport and the Regions

Driving Standards Agency

Every effort has been made to ensure that the information contained in
this publication is accurate at the time of going to press. The Stationery
Office cannot be held responsible for any inaccuracies. Information in
this book is for guidance only.

DSA THE CBT GUIDE

The Driving Standards Agency (DSA) is an executive agency of the Department of the Environment, Transport and the Regions. You'll see its logo at test centres.

'Safe driving for life'

The aim of DSA is to promote road safety through the advancement of driving standards.

DSA

- conducts practical driving tests for drivers or riders of cars, motorcycles, lorries, buses and other vehicles

- plans, maintains and supervises the theory test for drivers or riders of cars, motorcycles, lorries and buses

- controls the register of Approved Driving Instructors (ADIs)

- supervises Compulsory Basic Training (CBT) courses for motorcyclists

- aims to provide a high-quality service to its customers.

DSA THE CBT GUIDE

CONTENTS

DSA THE CBT GUIDE

The Government has long been concerned about the safety of motorcyclists. Over the years various pieces of legislation have been introduced to reduce two-wheeled-motor-vehicle casualties, including the compulsory wearing of safety helmets and restrictions on the size of learner motorcycles.

Compulsory Basic Training (CBT) was introduced in 1990 to equip new riders with basic skills before riding on the road. CBT isn't a test and there's no exam – it's a course of training you're required to complete satisfactorily. As a road safety initiative it has proved to be a great success and motorcycling today is safer than it has ever been.

This guide to CBT will show you what to expect from the course and help you keep track of your progress. How long you take to complete the course will depend on how quickly you pick it up.

Learning to ride a motorcycle is a continuous process, and CBT is just the beginning. Remember the lessons you learn here, practice them whenever you ride, and always put safety first.

Whenever you ride your aim must always be

'Safe driving for life'

Robin Cummins

Robin Cummins

**The Chief Driving Examiner
Driving Standards Agency**

This book will help you to

- **understand the purpose of CBT**

- **prepare for your CBT course**

- **follow your progress through the CBT course.**

Part One tells you what you need to know to begin CBT and outlines the modular content of the course.

Part Two explains the details of each module of the CBT course.

Part Three contains advice on how to continue your training after CBT and gives details about the theory and practical motorcycle test.

Part Four gives other useful information including addresses which may be helpful. There is also a personal CBT training record which you can use to keep track of your progress.

The important factors

CBT is just the beginning of your motorcycling career and this book is only one of the important factors in your training. Others are

- a good instructor

- a positive attitude

- patience and practice.

How you choose to develop as a motorcyclist is up to you. You should aim to be a safe and confident rider for life. Don't just put on a show for your test and then revert to a lower standard. Take pride in always setting a good example.

Riding safely is a life skill.

Books for study

It's strongly recommended that you study a copy of *The Highway Code* (The Stationery Office). You can order a copy when you apply for your licence or buy one from a good bookshop.

The DSA 'Driving Skills' series of books will provide you with sound knowledge of riding skills and safe riding practices. *The Official Theory Test for Car Drivers and Motorcyclists, The Motorcycling Manual,* and *The Driving Test* are all published by The Stationery Office.

A CD-ROM *The Theory Test and Beyond* (The Stationery Office) provides a fun and modern way of learning.

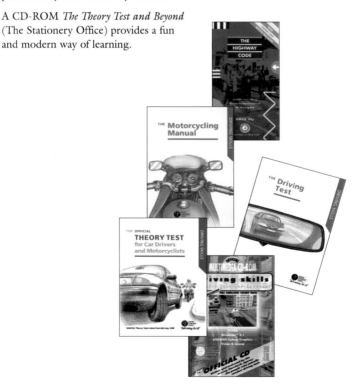

The topics covered

- What is CBT?

- CBT elements.

- CBT instructors.

- Getting started.

What is CBT?

Outline

CBT is a course of Compulsory Basic Training which all learner

- moped
- motorcycle

riders must complete before riding on the road.

CBT can only be given by Approved Training Bodies (ATBs) who have

- instructors that have been assessed by the DSA
- sites approved by DSA for off-road training

CBT is an opportunity to safely learn

- motorcycling theory
- skills which will make you safe on the road
- the correct attitude towards motorcycling.

Many people find CBT is an enjoyable activity and an opportunity to meet like-minded motorcyclists.

The CBT course

The course is broken down into five elements which will be worked through in order. The elements are

- Introduction
- Practical on-site theory
- Practical on-site training
- Practical on-road training
- Practical on-road riding.

The first four elements take place in safe off-road sites while the final element puts the theory and training into practice on the road.

When you have satisfactorily completed the course you'll be issued with a certificate of completion (DL196).

The DL196 is a legal document which

- is valid for three years from its date of issue
- validates your driving licence.

You will have to produce a valid DL196 before you can take the practical moped or motorcycle test.

If you complete CBT when you're 16 years old using a moped the DL196 obtained will remain valid for motorcycles when you reach the age of 17.

Note.

All DL196 certificates issued before 1 July 1996 begin their three-year life on that date.

Origins

The purpose of introducing CBT was to try and reduce the high levels of road accidents involving motorcyclists, particularly young and inexperienced riders.

Since 1990 there has been a dramatic reduction in motorcycle casualties. While other factors may have had an effect, the figures suggest that CBT has played a big part in achieving this reduction.

In 1997 the content of CBT was reviewed to ensure that it remained

- relevant
- comprehensive.

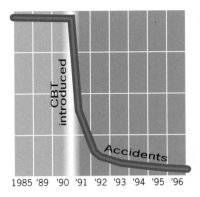

Who's affected

CBT was introduced for

- provisional licence holders in December 1990
- all learner moped and motorcycle riders in January 1997.

You don't have to take CBT if you

- have a full moped licence obtained by passing a moped test after 1 December 1990
- live and ride on specified offshore islands
- already hold a valid DL196 (obtained during a previous motorcycle entitlement or when riding a moped)
- wish to ride a moped using the full moped entitlement provided by a full car licence.

DSA THE CBT GUIDE

CBT elements

CBT is arranged so that you progress
through a series of elements. You will
only move onto the next element when
your instructor is satisfied you

- have learnt the necessary theory
- have demonstrated the practical skills
  to a safe basic level.

The elements are

- 'A' Introduction.
- 'B' Practical on-site training
- 'C' Practical on-site riding
- 'D' Practical on-road training
- 'E' Practical on-road riding.

The elements are described in detail in
Part Two.

Element order

The elements MUST be taken in the
order shown. Your instructor will ensure
you complete each element before you
progress to the next.

Within each element the instructor is free
to deliver the training in the order which
is felt to be most appropriate for you.

The CBT record in Part Four of this
book will allow you to record when each
of the elements has been completed.

Instructor-to-trainee ratios

During your CBT you may be
accompanied by other learners up to a
maximum ratio of

- 4:1 during on-site elements
- 2:1 during the on-road element.

For Direct Access the ratios are 2:1 for
both on- and off- road elements.

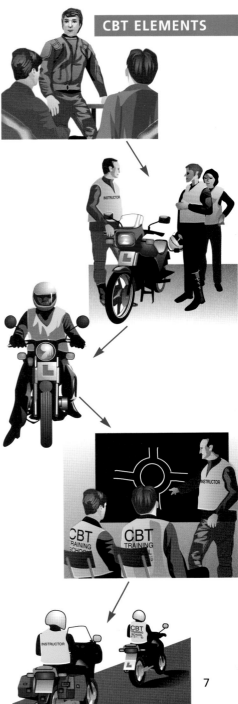

CBT Instructors

CBT is given by instructors who are either

- DSA Assessed Instructors
- Down-Trained Certified Instructors.
- Assistant Instructors.

DSA Assessed Instructors

Every ATB must employ at least one instructor who has successfully attended the DSA's CBT assessment course. They're called Cardington Assessed Instructors and can

- provide CBT training and issue DL196 certificates
- down-train other instructors within the ATB.

Down-Trained Certified Instructors

These instructors have been down-trained by the Cardington Assessed Instructor and are qualified to provide CBT training including issuing the DL196 certificate at the end of the course.

Assistant Instructors

An Assistant Instructor can deliver the off-road training elements, but is not entitled to carry out any on-road training or issue DL196 certificates.

Note. From January 1998 no more Assistant Instructors will be appointed.

Direct Access supervision

Some instructors may have a further qualification allowing them to give Direct Access supervision. This is obtained by attending DSA's Direct Access Scheme assessment course.

How can I tell which type of instructor is giving me training?

When training your instructor will be carrying with them their certificate. A certificate containing the letter C indicates a Cardington Assessed Instructor while a D indicates they are Direct Access qualified.

Quality control

DSA monitors the standard of training given by instructors. If a DSA examiner is present during your training, don't worry. The examiner

- will not take part in the training
- is there to safeguard the quality of training you receive.

Choosing an ATB

You can find out about the ATBs in your area from

- the local road safety officer
- most motorcycle dealers
- motorcycle papers and magazines
- local papers
- local Yellow pages.
- DSA Tel: 0115 901 2595

DSA THE CBT GUIDE

Getting started

Having decided to ride a motorcycle and planned to undergo CBT you need to consider the basic starting requirements.

Driving licence

To ride a motorcycle on the road you must be at least 17 years old and hold a driving licence which allows you to ride motorcycles (Category A).

As a learner motorcyclist this licence must provide provisional motorcycle entitlement and will be either

- a provisional driving licence with motorcycle entitlement
- full car licence, which automatically provides provisional motorcycle entitlement
- a full moped licence.

Provisional motorcycle entitlement

This entitles learners to ride a solo motorcycle after completing CBT

- up to 125cc
- with a power output of no more than 11kW.

Learners who wish to ride a sidecar outfit can do so as long as it has a power to weight ratio not exceeding 0.16kW/kg.

With provisional motorcycle entitlement you must not

- ride on motorways
- carry a pillion passenger
- ride without L plates. In Wales you may display a red D plate (for Dysgwr, the Welsh for learner). If you cross from Wales into another part of the United Kingdom you must display an L plate.

Two-year limit   Motorcycle entitlement on a provisional licence lasts for two years. You must pass the motorcycle test within that time or your entitlement will expire. You will then have to wait one year before you can apply for motorcycle entitlement again.

Moped riders   To ride a moped on the road you must be at least 16 years old and have a driving licence that entitles you to ride mopeds.(Category P)

At 16 but under 17 this can be a

- full moped licence
- provisional moped licence.

At 17 and over it can also be a

- full car or motorcycle licence (these provide full moped entitlement)
- provisional driving licence (this provides automatic provisional moped entitlement).

Provisional moped entitlement is not subject to the two-year limit and allows you to ride a machine which

- has an engine under 50cc
- has a maximum design speed not exceeding 30 mph
- doesn't weigh more than 250kg
- can be moved by pedals if the moped was registered before 1 August 1977.

Full moped entitlement allows you to ride mopeds without L plates and to carry a pillion passenger.

Full motorcycle licence

There are two types of full motorcycle licence

• Category A1

• Category A.

Category A1   A full category A1 licence allows you to ride machines up to 125cc and with a power output of up to 11kW (14.6 bhp).

The practical test must be taken on a bike of between 75cc and 125cc.

Category A   A full category A licence gives you full entitlement to all machines. You can obtain a full category A licence by

• passing the motorcycle test on a machine of over 120cc but no more than 125cc and capable of at least 100kph (62.5 mph).
  Note. Your full entitlement will be restricted to machines of 25kW (33 bhp) maximum for a two-year qualifying period.

• Direct Access. This route is for riders aged 21 or over and the test must be taken on a machine of at least 35kW (46.6 bhp)

• Accelerated Access. This route is for riders who are or become 21 years or over during the two year qualifying period. A second test must be taken on a machine of at least 35kW (46.6 bhp). (CBT doesn't have to be repeated.)

Motorcycle

As a new motorcyclist there are several options open to you at this stage.

You may

• buy a learner motorcycle

• hire a motorcycle for the CBT course and for training up to and including your L test

• choose the Direct Access route to a full licence if 21 or over

The option you choose can affect the type of full licence you obtain after passing the L test.

Buy a learner motorcycle   Learner motorcycles are

• up to 125cc

• with a maximum power output of 11kW (14.6 bhp).

If you use such a machine for your practical test you need to know that

• passing the test on a machine between 75cc and 125cc will entitle you to a full A1 licence

• passing the test on a machine of over 120cc but not more than 125cc and capable of at least 100kph (62.5 mph) you will be given a full category A licence. You will then be restricted to riding motorcycles with a maximum power of 25kW (33 bhp) for a two-year qualifying period.

Hire a motorcycle You can hire a machine for CBT from most training organisations. You may find you can also hire a motorcycle for additional training and for the practical test. Talk to local ATBs to find out what they can offer.

Direct Access If you are at least 21 years old you may decide to learn to ride a motorcycle using the Direct Access route.

Your CBT may be taken on a Direct Access motorcycle. Some of the initial parts however, may be covered around a standard learner machine.

The motorcycle you use for the Direct Access test must be at least 35kW (46.6 bhp).

Motorcycles suitable for Direct Access can usually be hired from your local ATB.

Clothing

Your instructor will discuss motorcycle clothing in detail as part of the course.

If you are just starting to ride it will pay you to listen to your instructor before rushing out to buy anything.

During your CBT you

• must wear the visibility aid provided by the ATB. This will carry the name of the training organisation

• should wear appropriate clothing and stout footwear.

Many ATBs provide basic equipment for the CBT course.

See Element A.

Insurance

If you hire equipment and the machine from the ATB they should provide the necessary insurance.

Insurance will be discussed in Element D.

PART TWO THE CBT ELEMENTS

INTRODUCTION TO CBT

The topics covered

- The aims of CBT.
- Equipment and clothing.
- Eyesight test.

The aims of Element A

This element is an introduction to CBT.

It will take the form of a discussion. Your instructor will explain the basics and not get involved in complicated issues.

Wherever possible your instructor will use examples to help demonstrate the point being made.

As a part of this element you'll have your entitlement to ride motorcycles checked. If necessary your instructor will explain what you need to do in order to obtain this entitlement.

At the end of this module you should understand the

- purpose of CBT
- the content of CBT.

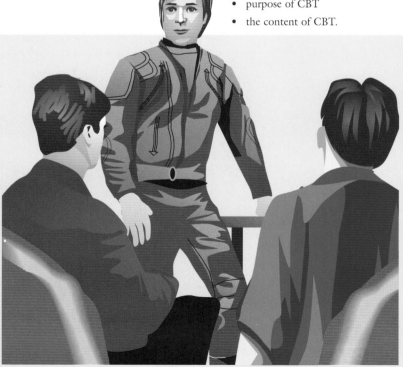

What CBT requires

You cannot ride on the road unaccompanied until you have satisfactorily completed all the elements of CBT.

Your instructor will explain the aims of CBT and will also explain why it was introduced.

An overview of the course content should be given.

The time it takes to complete the course will be determined by you. Your instructor should not move you on to the next part until you're ready.

Within each element instructors are free to deliver the topics in the order that they find best for you. Every topic must, however, be covered to the necessary level.

You'll need to demonstrate to your instructor that you have a basic skill level and an understanding of each topic. This may be through question and answer sessions for the theory or through practical demonstrations of your riding ability.

Points to remember

Don't treat CBT as a formality you must grudgingly endure.

Instructors are experienced motorcyclists who

- have valuable advice to give learner riders
- are motorcycle enthusiasts.

Take CBT seriously and enjoy learning safely.

Many experienced car drivers who take up motorcycling, find that CBT is an eye opening experience which

- increases their awareness of hazards
- gives them skills which improve their driving.

Element A

What CBT requires

Your instructor will explain the different types of motorcycle clothing available. As well as looking at outer clothing, the talk will include

- helmets
- visors and goggles
- gloves
- boots.

Motorcycle equipment is generally expensive and your instructor will help

- prioritise which equipment you should buy first
- identify less expensive alternatives.

You should also discuss

- the effects of getting cold and wet
- how some clothing can help protect from certain injuries.

Points to remember

You'll need to know

- the legal requirements for helmets
- how to fasten your helmet securely
- about the BSI Kitemark on visors and goggles

You must also know the dangers of riding

- with scratched, damaged and tinted visors or goggles.
- with a damaged helmet
- without eye protection
- without gloves
- in shorts
- in sandles or trainers
- without adequate clothing in bad weather.

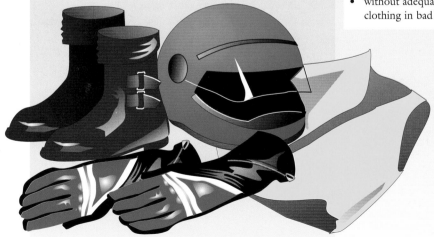

DSA THE CBT GUIDE

What CBT requires

At this stage in CBT your instructor will check your eyesight.

You must be able to read a number plate

- in good daylight
- with letters 79.4 mm (3.1 in) high
- at a distance of 20.5 m (about 67 feet)
- with the aid of glasses or contact lenses if necessary.

Your instructor will also check your driving licence entitlement to ride motorcycles.

If necessary you'll be advised on how to obtain motorcycle entitlement on your licence.

Points to remember

If you fail to reach the required standard in the eyesight test DSA will recommend that the remaining elements of the course should not proceed.

You **must** demonstrate that you can reach the required eyesight standard, using glasses or contact lenses if necessary, before Element E can be taken.

If you've demonstrated that you need to wear glasses or contact lenses to pass the eyesight test you **must** wear them whenever you ride on the road.

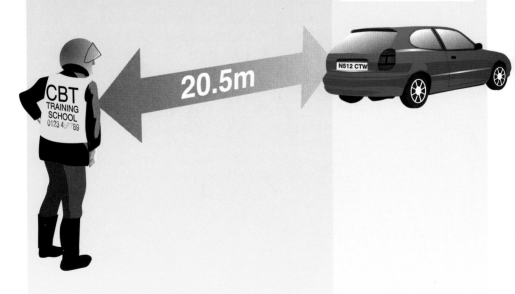

PRACTICAL ON-SITE TRAINING

The topics covered

- Motorcycles and their controls.

- Basic safety checks and use of the stands

- Wheeling the motorcycle and braking to stop.

- Starting and stopping the engine.

The aims of Element B

This element provides you with an introduction to the motorcycle.

You'll not start riding the motorcycle in this element although you'll get hands-on training.

At the end of the element you'll

- be able to show a working knowledge of the machine

- have a feel for the weight and balance of a motorcycle.

What CBT requires

Your instructor will show you around a motorcycle and will explain the controls in a logical order.

The controls covered will include

- Hand controls
- Foot controls
- Instruments

Hand controls

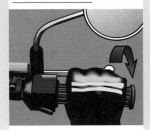

- throttle
- front brake
- clutch
- indicators
- choke
- electric starter
- engine kill switch
- lighting switches
- horn
- fuel tap.

Foot controls

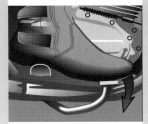

- rear brake
- kick starter
- gearchange lever.

Instruments

- speedometer
- rev. counter
- warning lamps.

Skills you'll acquire

Practise finding and using the controls. Some controls are adjustable. Your instructor will explain how they can be set up to suit you.

You'll also need to develop a feel for the controls. Remember that when riding you'll be wearing gloves and boots. This may affect the feel and ease with which you can reach certain controls.

Faults to avoid

It should not require great strength or force to operate the motorcycle's controls. Be especially careful with

- accelerator
- clutch
- brakes.

You must be able to operate the controls smoothly and without having to look down to find them.

Element B

What CBT requires

Your instructor will show you how to make basic checks to ensure your motorcycle is safe.

These checks will include

- the brakes for correct operation and adjustment
- the steering head for wear and adjustment
- control cables for wear, adjustment and lubrication
- fluid levels
  - hydraulic brake fluid
  - engine oil
  - coolant
  - battery electrolyte
- all lights
- suspension
- wheels and spokes
- tyres for wear, damage and pressure
- drive chain for wear, lubrication and tension
- nuts and bolts for tightness
- number plates and reflectors for visibility
- mirrors for clarity

You will also be shown the types of motorcycle stands and how and when to use them.

Skills you'll acquire

While you're not expected to become a motorcycle mechanic, you'll need to be able to recognise basic faults which could affect your motorcycle's roadworthiness.

When using the stands you need to

- demonstrate the correct techniques for putting a motorcycle onto and off its stands
- show an understanding of the effects of camber and gradient.

Faults to avoid

It's important that you know which machine checks you need to make on a daily basis and which can be left longer.

Make sure you can manage using the stands correctly. Incorrect methods of using the stands can lead to personal injury or damage to the machine.

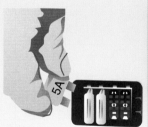

18

What CBT requires

You'll learn how to balance a motorcycle while wheeling it both to the left and right (in either order).

Your instructor will show you

- where to stand
- how to hold the motorcycle
- how to lean the motorcycle while wheeling it.

In addition you'll be taught how to use the front brake to stop in a controlled manner. This will involve

- making sure the motorcycle is upright
- practice to get the feel of the front brake.

Skills you'll acquire

You'll have to demonstrate

- full control of the motorcycle while wheeling it
- that you have the necessary balance skills.

Your instructor will want to see that you can squeeze the front brake gently and effectively to stop.

Faults to avoid

When wheeling the motorcycle avoid

- holding somewhere other than the handlebar grips
- wobbling
- insecure control
- harsh use of the front brake.

Element B

What CBT requires

Your instructor will show you what checks you need to make before starting the engine. A mnemonic such as PIGS may be used.

Petrol You'll be shown how to

- check for fuel in the tank
- turn on the petrol tap
- use the reserve position.

The use of the choke will also be explained.

Ignition You'll be shown

- the positions on the ignition switch
- how to switch on the ignition.

The ignition kill switch will be explained.

Gears This will cover checking for neutral by

- rocking the machine back and forward
- spinning the rear wheel on the stand
- checking the neutral lamp.

Start You should be shown how to use

- electric starters
- kick starters.

Skills you'll acquire

Before starting the engine you'll need to

- be able to find neutral and recognise a 'false neutral'
- demonstrate that you know how to operate the ignition switch and any immobiliser fitted
- know how to operate the starter mechanism fitted to your machine.

Faults to avoid

Before you start the engine don't forget to turn on the fuel. The engine may well start but will splutter and cut out before you've travelled far if you don't.

Only use the choke for the shortest period. Running with the choke on for longer than necessary can cause

- the engine to run too fast when you're trying to slow down
- increased wear on the engine
- more fuel to be used and more pollution produced.

When starting the engine

- make sure you have selected neutral
- don't hold the kick start lever down after the kick over
- don't hold the starter button on after the engine has started.

When stopping the engine don't

- use the kill switch unless in an emergency
- forget to switch off the fuel tap.

PRACTICAL ON-SITE RIDING

The topics covered

- Riding in a straight line and stopping.

- Riding slowly.

- Using the brakes.

- Changing gear.

- Riding a figure of eight.

- Emergency stopping.

- Rear observation.

- Turning left and right.

- U-turn.

The aims of Element C

In this element you'll begin riding a motorcycle.

By the time you've finished this element you'll have developed enough basic skills to allow you to ride a motorcycle under control.

You'll also learn the essential techniques you need for dealing with hazards including

- rear observation

- Observe–Signal–Manoeuvre (OSM) and the Position– Speed–Look (PSL) routines.

You will practise these practical skills until your instructor is satisfied that you'll be safe when you're taken out onto the road.

What CBT requires

This is the point in CBT where you begin riding a motorcycle.

Your instructor will explain and may also demonstrate what's required.

You'll be shown how to move off and how to stop. This will include

- using the clutch
- selecting first gear
- finding the 'biting point'
- using the brakes to stop.

Covering the rear brake will be explained to you and you'll be expected to put this into practice.

Your instructor will also show you how to ride in a straight line, including advice on how to keep your balance.

Skills you'll acquire

You'll need to practise until you can

- co-ordinate the controls when moving off and stopping
- keep your balance
- use both brakes in a smooth and controlled manner.

Faults to avoid

When you move off for the first time you may feel insecure. Avoid riding with your feet hanging down. From the beginning learn to ride with your feet up on the footrests.

When you stop you'll have to put a foot down to support the motorcycle. Your instructor will explain

- which foot to put down
- why that foot.

Follow the guidance and make sure you understand why.

Avoid fierce use of the controls at all times as this can lead to

- stalling the engine
- skidding
- loss of steering control.

What CBT requires

You'll have to show you can ride a motorcycle slowly and under full control. This is to prepare you for riding on the road where this skill will be needed to deal with

- junctions
- slow moving traffic in queues
- hazards.

A demonstration of what is required will probably be given to help show

- the level of control achievable
- how slowly you'll be expected to ride.

Skills you'll acquire

You'll need to demonstrate your skill in using the

- throttle
- clutch
- brakes

while keeping your

- balance
- steering

under control.

Faults to avoid

- Loss of balance.
- Loss of steering control.
- Harsh use of
  - throttle
  - clutch
  - brakes.
- Riding too fast.
- Not using the footrests.

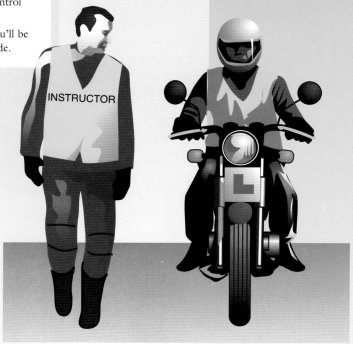

24

What CBT requires

You need to be able to operate the brakes in a controlled manner so that you can

- control your speed
- stop accurately.

You'll be shown how to use both brakes together for maximum control and stopping ability.

The importance of this skill can be related to the need to stop accurately at junctions.

Skills you'll acquire

Your instructor will expect you to stop the motorcycle at a marked position.

Cones, a line or some other marker may be used to identify where you are expected to stop.

Faults to avoid

- Not de-clutching as you stop.
- Use of the rear brake before the front.
- Use of one brake only.
- Harsh and late use the brakes.
- Locking the wheels.

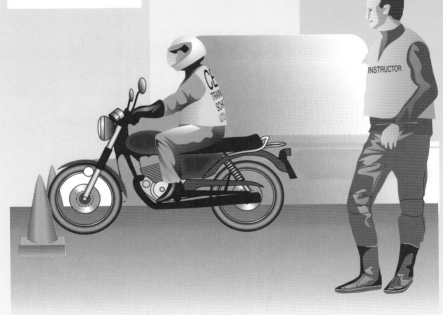

What CBT requires

You need to be able to change up and down smoothly through the gears.

Your instructor will explain how to operate the controls to achieve smooth gear changes.

The space on the training area may limit practice to second or third gear.

Skills you'll acquire

You'll need to demonstrate that you can

- co-ordinate the controls
- make upward and downward gear changes satisfactorily.

Faults to avoid

- Harsh use of the controls.
- Failing to co-ordinate clutch, throttle and gear change lever.
- Selecting the wrong gear.

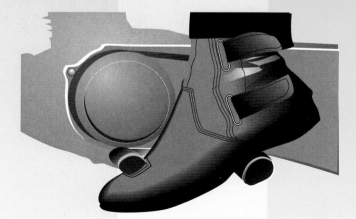

What CBT requires

This exercise is to develop steering and balance control when changing from one lock to another.

There are no set size measurements for this exercise. Your instructor may start off with a large layout and reduce it as your skill develops.

Skills you'll acquire

You will learn

- precise throttle control
- slow speed steering and balance control.

Faults to avoid

- Riding with your feet off the footrests.
- Harsh throttle and clutch control.
- Excessive speed.
- Wobbling.

What CBT requires

You must be able to stop safely should an emergency arise.

Your instructor will explain the effects of

- using the brakes individually
- using both brakes together.

This may then be followed by a demonstration to highlight the points.

You need to understand

- how weight is transferred during heavy braking
- how weight transfer can affect the rear wheel.

Reference may be made to using the brakes in the ratio 75% front and 25% rear. It's important to understand that this refers to braking pressure not lever movement.

The effects of weather conditions on this ratio will also need to be explained.

Skills you'll acquire

You must be able to co-ordinate front and rear brakes

- together
- in the correct ratio for the conditions.

Faults to avoid

- Late reactions when signalled to stop.
- Excessive brake pressure causing either or both wheels to lock.
- Not responding to the weather and road conditions.
- Not de-clutching as you stop.

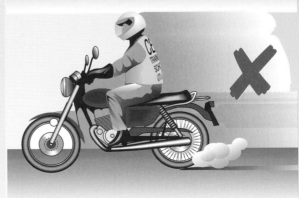

What CBT requires

To be safe on the road you should know as much about the traffic behind as you can.

On a motorcycle you can find out about traffic behind by

- using the mirrors
- turning and looking over your shoulder.

Your instructor will explain the special requirements for a motorcyclist including

- how and when using mirrors alone is not enough
- how to overcome the blind area.

You should practise looking round

- before moving off
- whilst on the move.

Skills you'll acquire

You'll need to practise looking round while moving so that

- you can see into the blind area
- rearward glances are kept as brief as possible.

Faults to avoid

- Looking round for an excessive time.
- Veering off course while looking round.
- Poorly timed rearward glances.

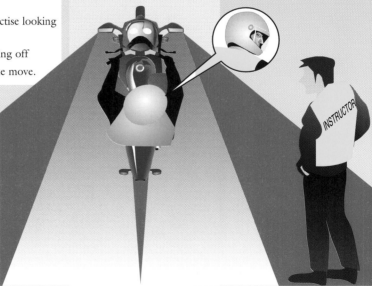

Element C

What CBT requires

You need to be able to deal safely with road junctions. Your instructor will explain the

- **O**bserve
- **S**ignal
- **M**anoeuvre
- **P**osition
- **S**peed
- **L**ook

procedure (**OSM/PSL**) and may give a demonstration.

The 'life saver' look will be explained.

An explanation of

- different junction types
- road markings
- traffic signals and signs

will be given.

You will need to know how to deal with left and right turns

- major to minor
- minor to major.

A mock junction layout may be set out on the training area for practice.

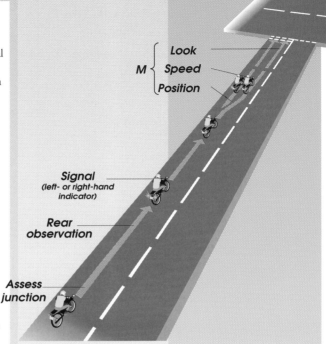

M { Look
    Speed
    Position

Signal
(left- or right-hand indicator)

Rear observation

Assess junction

Skills you'll acquire

Right and left turns require different procedures. You need to

- recognise the different types of turn
- demonstrate correct road positioning
- make effective observation
- give correct signals in good time.

Faults to avoid

- Making badly-timed rearward or sideways glances.
- Giving badly-timed or incorrect signals
- Looking around when the situation calls for concentration ahead.
- Not cancelling signals after turning.

DSA THE CBT GUIDE

What CBT requires

Riding a U-turn is a set exercise which also has practical use when riding on the road.

You need to be able to ride your motorcycle around in a U-turn

- under control
- with your feet on the footrests
- keeping aware of the traffic conditions.

Your instructor may demonstrate the level of

- balance
- steering
- clutch/throttle

control needed for this exercise.

You'll be given the chance to practise until you're confident in your ability.

Skills you'll acquire

To ride around in a U-turn you need to have developed your

- balance
- steering
- clutch/throttle

co-ordination and control.

In addition you need to understand

- when
- how
- where

to look for traffic or other hazards.

Faults to avoid

- Harsh use of the controls.
- Not taking effective observation.
- Using your feet to help overcome poor balance.

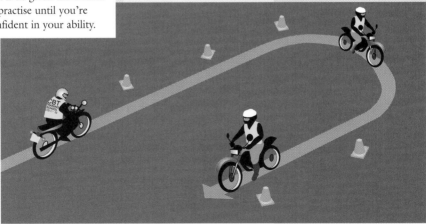

PRACTICAL ON-ROAD TRAINING

The topics covered

- Conspicuity.
- Legal requirements.
- Vulnerability.
- Speed.
- Highway Code.
- Anticipation.
- Rear observation.
- Road positioning.
- Separation distance.
- Weather conditions.
- Road surfaces.
- Alcohol and drugs.
- Attitude.
- Hazard perception.

The aims of Element D

Having carried out theory and practical training off-road your instructor will now prepare you for the on-road element of CBT.

The knowledge you gain now will be the foundations on which to build your motorcycling career.

This element will cover the information you need to ride

- legally
- safely

on the road.

During the on-road element aspects of this theory may be reinforced in practical situations.

What CBT requires

It is vitally important to understand why you need to be conspicuous when riding a motorcycle.

Your instructor will discuss the reasons for not being seen and how you can make it easy for others to see you

The talk will include

- visibility aids
- differences between
  - fluorescent materials
  - reflective materials
- use of headlights
- road positioning
- clothing
- keeping your motorcycle clean.

In addition there will be some discussion on the legal requirements to use dipped headlights in poor visibility.

Points to remember

Making yourself conspicuous is not a legal requirement. However it's in your own interest to make yourself easy to see. To do so avoid

- wearing dull clothing
- riding a dirty motorcycle
- riding in another road users blind area.

Element D

What CBT requires

Before you ride on the road there are minimum legal requirements you must be aware of.

Your instructor will explain about

- road tax
- insurance
- MOT certificates
- provisional motorcycle licence entitlement
- DL196 (CBT completion certificate)
- L plates.

In addition you need to know about

- general roadworthiness
- the legal requirement to fasten your helmet correctly.

Points to remember

Make sure you have all the legal aspects in order before riding on the road. You'll not always be sent a reminder when certain mandatory items need renewal/expire such as

- MOT certificates
- motorcycle licence entitlement
- DL196 certificates.

Don't get caught out through neglecting to keep everything up to date.

DSA THE CBT GUIDE

What CBT requires

As a motorcyclist you're generally more vulnerable than motorists.

Your instructor will explain about the dangers of

- falling off
- collision, even at low speed
- weather conditions
- road surface conditions.

The head and limbs are the most exposed parts of your body when riding. Your instructor will tell you what steps you can take to protect yourself from injury and the effects of the weather.

Points to remember

Always buy the best protective equipment you can afford.

Don't

- use a
  - damaged
  - second hand
  - poor fitting
  - unfastened
  helmet
- ride without protective clothing
- ride too fast for the conditions.

What CBT requires

You need to understand why riding at the correct speed is so important.

Riding too slow can be just as much a problem as riding too fast.

Your instructor will explain about the

- legal speed limits
- suitable use of speed
- consequences of
  - speeding
  - riding too slowly

Points to remember

You need to develop a defensive riding style so that you can always stop

- within your range of vision
- in case a potential hazard turns into a real danger.

Always ride within

- speed limits
- your ability.

DSA THE CBT GUIDE

What CBT requires

As a road user you should own a copy of the current *Highway Code* and refer to it often.

Without knowledge of *The Highway Code* you will find it difficult to deal with all aspects of training.

While *The Highway Code* contains **all** the essential elements of road safety, specific elements relating to CBT will be covered in more detail by your instructor.

Points to remember

Don't treat *The Highway Code* as a book to learn just for your driving test. It contains a wealth of information and advice which is designed to keep you safe whenever you use the road.

Refer to it often and follow the advice it gives.

What CBT requires

At all times you should ride defensively and anticipate the actions of other road users.

Your instructor will explain that to anticipate you need to

- look well ahead
- plan ahead
- develop hazard awareness
- concentrate at all times.

During discussion your instructor will cover a variety of scenarios which illustrate the point being made.

Points to remember

Anticipation is a skill which develops over time. Signs which show a lack of anticipation include

- late and harsh braking
- being distracted
- not taking road and weather conditions into account.

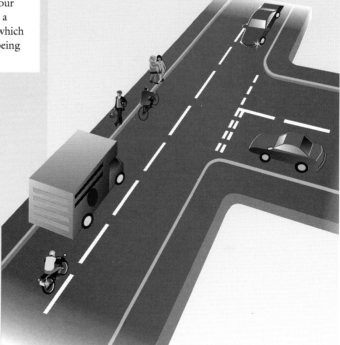

DSA THE CBT GUIDE

What CBT requires

You must understand that rear observation is a combination of

- using the mirrors
- looking around.

Your instructor will explain about

- effective rear observation
- timing of rearward glances.

Some time may be spent discussing the effects of looking around at the wrong moment.

Points to remember

Take care not to

- veer off course while looking round
- look round too late
- look round when you should be concentrating ahead.

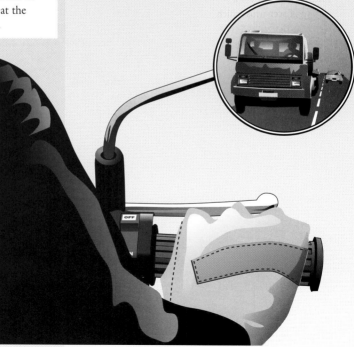

Element D

What CBT requires

It's important that you understand where you should position yourself when riding on the road.

Points which will be covered include how you should position yourself to deal with

- bends
- junctions
- road conditions
- single and dual carriageways
- hazards
- overtaking.

Points to remember

When you ride on the road always concentrate and avoid

- riding in the gutter
- erratic steering and veering across your lane
- failing to return to your normal position after dealing with a hazard
- riding in the crown of the road as a normal position.

DSA THE CBT GUIDE

What CBT requires

You must understand the importance of leaving sufficient space when following another vehicle.

This will involve discussing the advantages of allowing plenty of space such as

- increased ability to see past vehicles ahead and so allow for better forward planning
- increased likelihood of being seen by other road users.

The 'two-second rule' will be explained, and how this is affected by road and weather conditions should be covered.

The special requirements for following large vehicles will also be discussed.

Points to remember

Always keep the correct separation distance from the vehicle ahead.

It's important to allow for the

- effect road and weather conditions have on your stopping distance
- blind area of large vehicles.

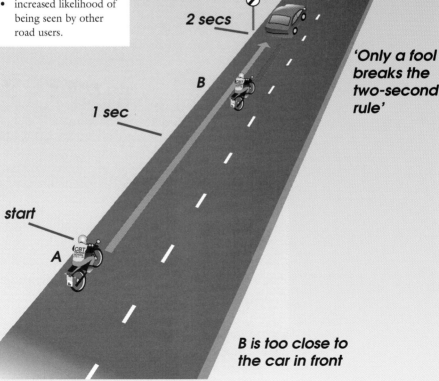

2 secs

B

1 sec

'Only a fool breaks the two-second rule'

start

A

B is too close to the car in front

Element D

What CBT requires

Motorcyclists are affected more by weather conditions than most other road users.

You can expect some discussion on how

- wind
- rain
- fog
- ice
- snow and sleet

affect motorcyclists.

In addition your instructor will explain how these weather conditions affect

- oil spillage
- painted road markings
- drain covers.

There should be discussion on turbulence caused by large vehicles and the effect that buffeting can have on motorcyclists.

Points to remember

During your training you are unlikely to encounter many adverse weather conditions.

When you do find yourself having to ride in bad weather conditions remember the advice your instructor has given.

Always respect the effects weather can have when you're riding a motorcycle.

If in doubt, don't set out !

DSA THE CBT GUIDE

What CBT requires

You need to be aware of how road conditions can affect a motorcyclist.

There are a variety of road surface hazards which will be explained including

- mud and leaves
- gravel and chippings
- tram and railway lines
- studs
- road markings
- drain covers
- shiny surfaces at junctions and roundabouts.

Clues which can help new riders will be discussed, such as

- rainbow colourings on a wet road indicating oil or fuel spillage
- 'Loose Chippings' road signs
- mud near farm and field entrances.

Points to remember

When you're riding always take the road conditions into account, especially when

- cornering
- accelerating
- braking.

Element D

What CBT requires

Alcohol

You are required to know that it's a criminal offence to ride with more than the legal level of alcohol in your blood.

Your instructor will make it clear that despite legally accepted limits, if you want to be safe and you're going to ride

DON'T DRINK AT ALL

Drugs

Taking certain drugs when you are going to drive is a criminal offence.

Your instructor will cover

- the effect drugs can have on concentration
- over the counter medicines
- how to check whether any medication will affect your riding ability
- how insurance policies could be invalidated.

Points to remember

Always

AVOID RIDING WHEN UNDER THE INFLUENCE OF ALCOHOL AND/OR DRUGS.

THE EFFECTS COULD BE
FATAL

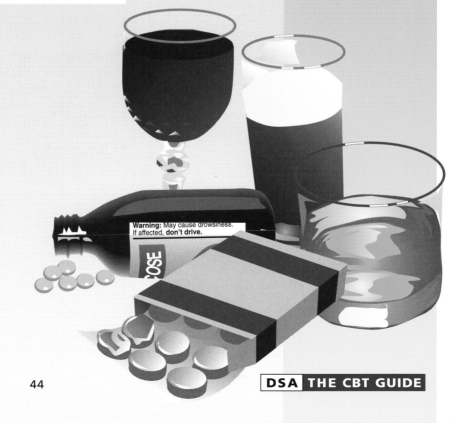

Warning: May cause drowsiness. If affected, **don't drive.**

What CBT requires

Your instructor will explain how your attitude can affect your safety. The points raised should include the

- effects of riding while angry
- importance of showing patience
- benefits of riding defensively.

Points to remember

Your attitude is under your control. You could put yourself at additional risk by

- riding while upset or angry
- riding in a spirit of competition on the road
- giving offence or provoking reaction by creating dangerous situations.

What CBT requires

You will be given some idea of what is meant by a hazard.

Your instructor will explain

- the importance of planning ahead
- how early recognition makes hazards easier to deal with
- the need for concentration
- the need to use all your your senses
- the importance controlling speed has in dealing with hazards.

Points to remember

Always keep up to date with the constantly changing road and traffic situations by

- concentrating at all times
- looking well ahead.

DSA THE CBT GUIDE

PRACTICAL ON-ROAD RIDING

The topics covered

- Traffic lights.

- Roundabouts.

- Junctions.

- Pedestrian crossings.

- Gradients.

- Bends.

- Obstructions.

- U-turn.

- Stopping as in an emergency.

The aims of Element E

This is the final element of the CBT course.

You'll ride out on the road

- accompanied by and in radio contact with a certified instructor *

- possibly with one other trainee

- for at least two hours.

You'll have to demonstrate that you can cope safely with a variety of road and traffic conditions.

Expect your instructor to stop now and again to

- discuss some aspect of your riding

- explain how to put the theory into practice.

Your ride should cover the topics discussed in this element of the book. (Some may not be covered due to the limits of the location.)

Your riding will be constantly assessed by your instructor.

A certificate of completion (DL196) will only be issued when the instructor is satisfied you're safe to continue learning alone.

* Special arrangements will be available for the deaf or hard of hearing.

What CBT requires

You must know how to act at traffic lights.

Apart from knowing the sequence of lights you need to know

- what the colours mean
- how to approach green lights safely
- how to cope with filter lanes
- what to do if traffic lights fail.

You'll also need to know about school crossing warning lights.

Skills you'll acquire

You must be able to

- approach traffic lights at the correct speed
- react to the road and weather conditions
- react correctly to changing lights.

Faults to avoid

- Failing to stop at a red light.
- Approaching green traffic lights too fast.
- Proceeding into the junction when the green light shows but the way isn't clear.
- Hesitating as the green light changes and stopping unsafely.

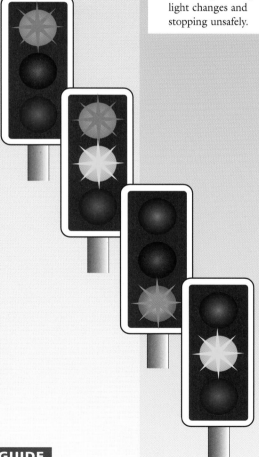

Element

E

What CBT requires

There are set procedures for dealing with roundabouts.

Your instructor should discuss and demonstrate how to go

- left
- ahead
- right.

This will involve learning how to apply the OSM/PSL routine for the direction you intend to travel. This will include

- signalling procedures
- lane discipline
- observation.

Your instructor will want to see you use safely the correct procedures for each roundabout you deal with.

Skills you'll acquire

You must be able to

- take effective rear observation
- approach at the correct speed
- give the correct signals at the right time
- follow the correct road position throughout
- judge the speed of other traffic
- cancel signals correctly.

Faults to avoid

- Giving wrong or misleading signals.
- Approaching at the wrong speed.
- Stopping when the way is clear.
- Positioning incorrectly.
- Riding out into the path of approaching traffic.
- Failing to take effective observation.

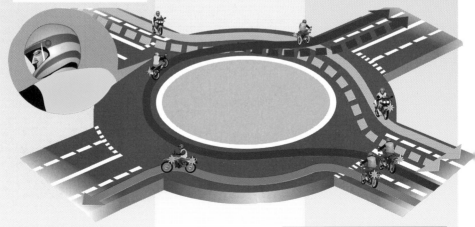

DSA THE CBT GUIDE

What CBT requires

You'll have practised turning left and right in Element C. You'll now have to combine those riding skills with real traffic situations.

Your instructor will want to see you deal with a variety of junctions. These may include

- crossroads
- T-junctions
- staggered junctions
- Y-junctions.

You'll be expected to react to signs such as

- warning signs
- STOP signs
- direction signs
- NO ENTRY signs
- priority signs

and road markings.

You must show you're aware of other road users and watch for vehicles approaching, emerging or turning.

Skills you'll acquire

To deal safely with junctions you must

- use the OSM/PSL routine correctly as you approach a junction
- position yourself correctly on the road
- control your speed to suit the road, weather and traffic conditions
- obey road signs and markings
- react correctly to other road users
- demonstrate effective observation.

Faults to avoid

All junctions must be treated with great care. Avoid

- stopping or waiting unnecessarily
- approaching a junction too fast
- overtaking as you approach a junction
- riding into a junction unsafely
- incorrect use of signals
- incorrect road position.

The road surface at junctions is often an additional hazard for motorcyclists. If you're riding on a shiny surface don't

- brake fiercely
- accelerate harshly.

What CBT requires

There's a variety of pedestrian crossings you can encounter.

- Zebra.
- Pelican.
- Toucan.
- Puffin.

Your instructor will want to see you

- at a zebra crossing
  - slow down and be prepared to stop for waiting pedestrians

- at pelican, puffin and toucan crossings
  - stop if the red light shows
  - give way to pedestrians on a pelican crossing when the amber lights are flashing
  - give way to cyclists on a toucan crossing, as you would to pedestrians.

Skills you'll acquire

As you approach a pedestrian crossing you need to

- control your speed
- react correctly to pedestrians waiting to cross
- know how and why you would give an arm signal as you stop at a zebra crossing.

Faults to avoid

- Approaching a crossing too fast.
- Failing to stop or show awareness of waiting pedestrians.
- Stopping across a crossing so blocking the way for pedestrians.
- Overtaking within the zigzag lines leading up to a crossing.
- Waving pedestrians across the road.
- Failing to respond correctly to traffic light signals at controlled crossings.

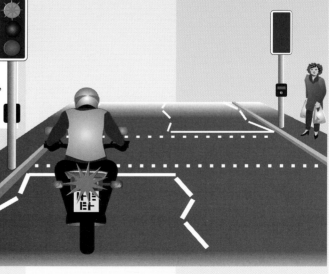

What CBT requires

During this element your instructor will want to see that you can cope with gradients.

This will entail

- hill start procedures
- riding uphill
- riding downhill.

You should have some understanding of how riding uphill or downhill can affect control of your motorcycle.

Skills you'll acquire

To move off on an uphill gradient you need to have good control of the

- clutch
- throttle.

When riding down a steep hill you need to know how to control your speed using the

- brakes
- gears

When riding up a steep hill you need to be able to match the gear to the speed and load on the engine.

Faults to avoid

When moving off don't

- move off into the path of passing traffic
- stall the engine
- roll backwards.

Element
E

What CBT requires

Any bend can be a hazard. You must be able to recognise the hazard and safely deal with it.

Your instructor will want to see that you

- ride at a speed such that you can stop within the distance you can see
- keep to the correct road position
- are aware of road surface hazards such as
  - drain covers
  - loose surfaces
  - adverse camber.

On left hand bends you will have less view ahead. Be prepared for

- pedestrians
- stopped or broken down vehicles
- cyclists
- stopped vehicles waiting to turn right.

You should know how the weather affects your safety when cornering.

Skills you'll acquire

To help you assess any bend you should be looking out for

- road signs
- road markings
- chevrons.

Approaching a bend you need to

- control your speed
- select the correct gear
- leave a safe gap between you and other vehicles.

You must be able to lean into a bend while steering a steady course.

Faults to avoid

- Coasting.
- Braking while leaning over.
- Cornering too fast.
- Leaning over too far.
- Riding in the wrong position
  - too close to oncoming traffic
  - too close to the gutter.

DSA THE CBT GUIDE

What CBT requires

Obstructions are another hazard you will need to deal with.

To deal safely with these your instructor will want to see that you're riding defensively.

That's always riding

- at the correct speed for the road, weather and traffic conditions
- in the correct position
- in the correct gear
- looking ahead, anticipating and preparing for changing situations.

Skills you'll acquire

How well you cope with an obstruction depends largely on how well you plan ahead. To cope with hazards you need to be

- looking well ahead
- giving yourself time and space to react
- using the OSM/PSL routine
- in the correct position
- in full control of your speed.

Your attitude can affect how easily you learn these skills.

Faults to avoid

- Failing to look far enough ahead.
- Reacting too late.
- Riding too fast.
- Approaching an obstruction in the wrong gear.

What CBT requires

As part of Element C you practised riding a U-turn on the training area.

During this element you'll be expected to ride a U-turn on the road.

This

- builds on the skills you learned earlier
- helps prepare you for your practical motorcycle test.

Your instructor will find a quiet side road and explain what's required.

You cannot complete Element E until your instructor is satisfied you can safely ride a U-turn on the road.

Skills you'll acquire

You'll need the machine control skills of

- balance
- steering
- clutch/throttle.

You'll have to develop these skills to include coping with

- the camber of the road
- the possibility of passing traffic
- kerbs on either side.

Faults to avoid

- Failure to take effective observation before or during the exercise.
- Riding into the kerb or onto the pavement.
- Using your feet to help balance.
- Harsh, clumsy use of the clutch and throttle.

What CBT requires

You've learnt and practised this exercise in Element C.

In this element you repeat the exercise but in an on road situation. This will

- develop your earlier skills
- help ensure your safety if an emergency does arise
- prepare you for performing this exercise on your practical motorcycle test.

Your instructor will find a quiet side road and explain the signal to be used.

You'll then be expected to ride at normal speed before being given the signal to stop.

At no time will your instructor let you ride off out of sight.

Skills you'll acquire

- Quick reaction to the stop signal.
- Use of both brakes in the appropriate ratio.
- The ability to quickly correct a locked wheel.

Faults to avoid

- Riding too slowly before the signal.
- Taking rear observation before reacting to the stop signal.
- Locking one or both wheels and failing to correct the fault.
- Stopping too slowly.
- Moving off unsafely after stopping.

The topics covered

- Further training
- The theory test
- The practical test

Further training

CBT will give you the foundations on which to build a safe motorcycling career. Like all new skills you need

- training
- practice

to become good at them.

Training

Many ATBs provide additional training up to practical test standard. Sometimes they can also book your practical test appointment at the local driving test centre.

You need to bear in mind

- the three-year life of the DL196 certificate
- the two-year life of motorcycle entitlement on a provisional licence
- the two-year life on a theory test pass certificate.

Ask your instructor about further training and make sure they cover the full syllabus, which can be found in *The Driving Test*.

Practise

- On as many different types of road as you can.
- In all sorts of traffic conditions – even in the dark.
- On dual carriageways where the upper speed limit applies.

You may be asked to drive on such roads during the test. Don't just concentrate on the exercises included in the test.

When you practise try not to

- obstruct other traffic. Most drivers are tolerant of learners, but don't try their patience too much
- annoy local residents. For example, by practising emergency stops in quiet residential streets or by practising on test routes.

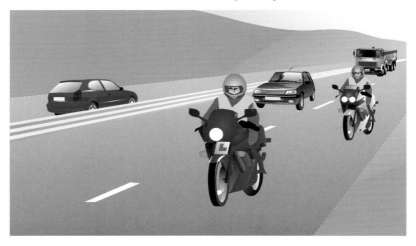

The theory test

Before you take your practical driving test you'll have to pass a theory test.* The theory test is straightforward and you'll pass if you're well prepared. You need to have a knowledge of *The Highway Code* and understand the principles of road safety.

How do I learn the theory?

It's important that you study the theory **at the same time** as learning the practical skills.

To help you learn the theory you should study *The Highway Code* . You can order a copy when you apply for your provisional licence.

Other study aids include

- books
- videos
- CD-ROMs
- mock theory test papers.

The Stationery Office produce a range of titles shown at the front of this book. These are available from

- booksellers
- by phoning The Stationery Office order line listed inside the back cover of this book.

***Note.**

You will not have to take a theory test if you hold a

- full car licence
- full moped licence obtained by passing both a theory and practical test.

How do I book a theory test?

Application forms are available from

- theory test centres
- driving test centres
- some ATBs.

The easiest way to book a test is by telephone, using your credit or debit card. If you book by this method you'll be given the date and time of your test immediately. You can do this by calling 0645 000 666 at any time between 8am and 6pm Monday to Friday. When you phone you should have ready your

- driving licence number
- credit or debit card details.

If you're deaf and need a minicom machine ring 0645 700 301.

Welsh speakers can ring 0645 700 201.

You'll be given a booking number. Take this together with your signed driving licence and photo identity (see page 62) when you attend your theory test.

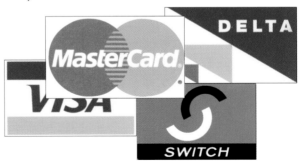

At the test centre

Make sure that you have all the necessary documents with you. You'll need

- your signed driving licence
- your appointment card or booking number
- photographic identity.

Photographic identity

The forms of photographic identification acceptable at both theory and practical tests are as follows

- **your passport** – this doesn't have to be a British passport
- **cheque guarantee card or credit card** with a signature and photograph of the candidate
- **an employer's identity or workplace pass** with candidate's photograph and their name or signature or both
- **a Trade Union Card** with candidate's photograph and signature
- **a Student Union Card** with reference to either the NUS or an education establishment/course reference number and displaying the candidate's photograph or signature or both
- **a School Bus Pass** with the name of the issuing authority and a photograph and signature of the candidate

- **a card issued in connection with sale and purchase of reduced price railway tickets** with the name of the issuing authority, that is, a card issued by a Railway Authority or other authorised body to purchase a reduced price railway ticket (e.g., a Young Persons Railcard).
- **a Gun Licence**, including a Firearm or Shotgun Certificate which bears the photgraph and signature of the candidate
- **a Proof of Age Card** issued by the Portman Group with the candidate's photograph and signature
- **a Standard Acknowlegement Letter (SAL)** issued by the Home Office with photograph and signature of the candidate.

No photo
No licence
No test

If you don't have any of these you can bring a photograph, together with a statement that it's a true likeness of you. This can be signed by any of the following

- DSA-certified motorcycle instructor
- Approved Driving Instructor
- Member of Parliament
- medical practitioner
- local authority councillor
- teacher (qualified)
- Justice of the Peace
- civil servant (established)
- police officer
- bank official
- minister of religion
- barrister or solicitor
- Commissioned Officer in Her Majesty's Forces.

I_____(name of certifier), certify that this is a true likeness of_____, who has been known to me for (number) months / years in my capacity as
_____

Signed _____
Dated _____
Daytime phone no. _____
ADI/CBT Instructor no. _____

If you don't bring these documents on the day you won't be able to take your test and you'll lose your fee. If you have any queries about what photographic evidence we will accept, contact the enquiry line.

Arrive in plenty of time so that you aren't rushed. The test centre staff will check your documents and ensure that you have the right category test paper to complete. If you arrive after the session has started you'll not be allowed to sit the test.

If you pass

If you pass you'll be

- notified of the result within two weeks

- issued with a pass certificate.

A same day results service has been introduced at selected theory test centres. An additional fee is charged for this service.

If you fail

If you don't pass the theory test you must retake and pass it before taking the practical test.

The pass certificate

The pass certificate will be valid for two years. You must take and pass the practical test within that time or you'll have to take the theory test again.

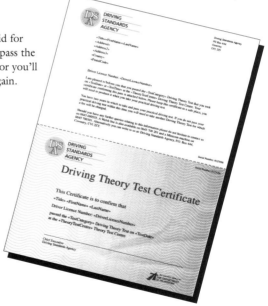

The practical test

How will I know when I'm ready for the practical test?

You must be able to ride

- consistently well and with confidence
- without assistance and guidance from your instructor

If you can't, you aren't ready for the test. Waiting until you are ready will save you time and money.

If you have taken additional training be guided by your instructor who has the knowledge and experience to tell you when you're ready.

Applying for a practical motorcycle test

You can apply for a practical test by

- post
- telephone.

To apply by post fill out an application form, DL 26 which is available from any

- DSA Area Office
- Driving Test Centre.

Full details of all fees can be obtained from DSA Area Offices or any Driving Test Centre.

Send your application to DSA at Newcastle. Complete the form and send it with the appropriate fee to the PO box and postcode for your area. Your application may be delayed if you address it incorrectly.

To book your test appointment over the telephone call the appropriate booking line. You'll find the telephone numbers in the back of this book. DSA accepts most major credit and debit cards.

If you wish to take your test in Wales using the Welsh language, please indicate this on the form.

Apply well before you want to be tested and give the earliest date you think you'll be ready.

You must show your CBT certificate to the examiner when you attend for your test. If you fail to do so your test will not be conducted.

Your test appointment

Your DSA Area Office will send you an appointment card. This will give you

- the time and date of the appointment
- the address of the Driving Test Centre
- other important information.

You should normally receive notification within two weeks of your application. If you don't, contact the DSA Area Office without delay.

Postponing your test appointment

Contact the DSA Area Office where you booked your test if

- the date or time on the card is not suitable
- you want to postpone or cancel the test.

You must give at least ten clear working days notice (that is two weeks – longer if there is a bank holiday) not counting

- the day the Office received your request
- the day of the test.

If you don't give enough notice, you will lose your fee.

Saturday and evening tests

Tests are availble at some driving test centres on Saturdays and weekday evenings. These tests have a higher fee.

Attending

Make sure you bring with you

- your signed driving licence; you will have to show it to your examiner and sign a declaration that your machine is insured

- your CBT certificate – your examiner will have to see the certificate before the test can begin

- photo identity – the same identity acceptable for the theory test is acceptable for the practical test.

Impersonating a driving test candidate is a crime. It is up to you to satisfy the examiner of your identity. If you cannot, your test will not be conducted.

Your test motorcycle

Make sure that the motorcycle you intend to ride during your test is

- legally roadworthy and has a current MOT test certificate, if it is over the prescribed age

- fully covered by insurance for its present use and for you to ride

- of the correct engine size/power output for the category of test you are taking

- properly licensed with the correct tax disc displayed

- displaying L-plates, (or D plates in Wales) which are visible from the front and rear.

If you overlook any of these your test may be cancelled and you could lose your fee.

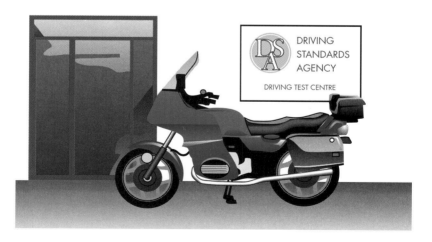

DS
A
DRIVING
STANDARDS
AGENCY
DRIVING TEST CENTRE

Disabilities or special circumstances

To make sure that enough time is allowed for your test, it would help DSA to know if you

- are deaf or have severe hearing difficulties
- are in any way restricted in your movements
- have any disability which may affect your riding.

If any one of these apply to you, please write this on your application form.

If you can't speak English or are deaf, you're allowed to bring an interpreter (who must not be your instructor). The interpreter must be at least 16 years of age.

DSA THE CBT GUIDE

This part lists

- DSA addresses

- other addresses you may find useful

- training record

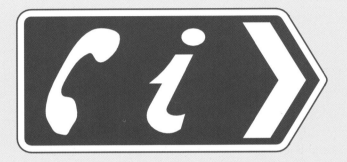

DSA addresses

Head Office

Stanley House
Talbot Street
Nottingham
NG1 5GU

Tel: 0115 901 2500

Theory test booking

To book a theory test either

- send a completed application to the address on the form

or

- book by telephone on 0645 000 666

Practical test booking

To book a practical driving test either

- send a completed application form to the appropriate Area Office.

or

- use the telephone booking facility calling the appropriate booking number.

London and the South-East

DSA
PO Box 289
Newcastle-upon-Tyne
NE99 1WE

Telephone bookings by credit card and other enquiries

Tel: 0171 957 0957
Fax: 0171 468 4550
Recorded message:
0171 468 4530

Midlands and Eastern

DSA
PO Box 287
Newcastle-upon-Tyne
NE99 1WB

Telephone bookings by credit card and other enquiries

Tel: 0121 697 6700
Fax: 0121 697 6750
Recorded message:
0121 697 6730

Wales and Western

DSA
PO Box 286
Newcastle-upon-Tyne
NE99 1WA

Telephone bookings by credit card and other enquiries

Tel: 0122 258 1000
Fax: 0122 258 1050
Recorded message:
0122 258 1030

Northern

DSA
PO Box 280
Newcastle-upon-Tyne
NE99 1FP

Telephone bookings by credit card and other enquiries

Tel: 0191 201 4000
Fax: 0191 201 4010
Recorded message:
0191 201 4100

Scotland

DSA
PO Box 288
Newcastle-upon-Tyne
NE99 1WD

Telephone bookings by credit card and other enquiries

Tel: 0131 529 8580
Fax: 0131 529 8589
Recorded message:
0131 529 8592

Other addresses you may find useful

Driver and Vehicle Licensing Agency (DVLA)

Customer Enquiry Unit
Swansea SA6 7JL

Tel: 0179 277 2151

The Royal Society for the Prevention of Accidents (RoSPA)

Edgebaston Park
353 Bristol Road
Birmingham B5 7ST

Tel: 0121 248 2000
Fax: 0121 248 2001

You can use this log to record your progress through CBT. As you successfully complete each element get your instructor to sign this progress record. This will give you

- a record of when you successfully complete each element
- a record of your instructor
- evidence of your progress to date.

CBT training record

Name . . . .

has satisfactorily completed

Element A of CBT.   Signed . . . .   Date . . . .

Element B of CBT.   Signed . . . .   Date . . . .

Element C of CBT.   Signed . . . .   Date . . . .

Element D of CBT.   Signed . . . .   Date . . . .

Element E of CBT.   Signed . . . .   Date . . . .

for . . . . ATB

DSA THE CBT GUIDE

*Essential reading from the **Driving Standards Agency***

Prepare for the driving tests wit

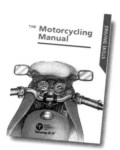

The Official Theory Test for Car Drivers and Motorcyclists 1998-1999 edition

Completely updated to include the new enlarged question bank (effective from July 1998). Essential reading for all new learner drivers, this is the only official theory test title written and compiled by the DSA.

c400 PAGES ILLUSTRATED IN FULL COLOUR
ISBN 0 11 552017 1
PAPERBACK   £11.99

The Driving Manual

Covering everything that the driver needs to know about good driving techniques for today's challenging driving conditions.

336 PAGES ILLUSTRATED IN FULL COLOUR
ISBN 0 11 551782 0
PAPERBACK   £12.99

The Motorcycling Manual

The authoritative guide to motorcycling, containing new graphics and photos. An essential reference book for motorcyclists who are keen to improve their machine handling and safety skills.

176 PAGES ILLUSTRATED IN FULL COLOUR
ISBN 0 11 551781 2
PAPERBACK   £9.99

Test Yourself Papers for the Driving Theory Test

Five practice papers for the theory test, with questions taken from the official question bank and the correct answers supplied for further reference and revision.

ISBN 0 11 551984 X
£4.99 (INCL VAT)

the official guidance ...

Know Your Traffic Signs

The best-selling booklet which aims to illustrate and explain the vast majority of
traffic signs which any road user is likely to encounter.
100 pages illustrated in colour

ISBN 0 11 551612 3
£2.50

The Driving Test

Advice on the practical test - from the official syllabus, preparation, test requirements, skills to be acquired and faults to avoid.

ISBN 0 11 551778 2
£4.99

New ways to take your test
Preview the theory test by telephone, online and on CD-ROM

The Audio Mock Theory Test

Devised to simulate the real theory test, this telephone service gives
results - with 4 papers to choose from, each containing 35 questions.

Call 0930 2-4-4-8-4-8

*(Calls cost 50p per minute; each paper takes approx 30 minutes to complete;
callers must be 18 or over)*

cyberdrive – the new web site for learner drivers

Visit our new online site for everything you need to know to help you to pass your
theory and practical tests, and to help you to advance your driving skills. Including
the new online mock theory test - which simulates the real test and gives immediate
results.

http://www.cyberdrive.co.uk

Driving Skills: Theory Test and Beyond on CD-Rom – See overleaf for details.

Order Form

These titles are available from:

- **The Publications Centre, PO Box 276, London SW8 5DT**
  Mail or Fax this order form or telephone.
  Telephone orders: 0171 873 9090 quoting ref 984
  Fax orders: 0171 873 8200
  General enquiries: 0171 873 0011

- **Online**
  Stationery Office publications are also available from our
  Virtual Bookstore: **http://www.national-publishing.co.uk**

- **The Stationery Office Bookshops**
  (See inside back cover for details)

- **Accredited Agents and all good bookshops
  and multimedia retailers**
  Handling charge: £2.50 per order

Please send me the following titles:

Title	ISBN	Quantity	Price
The Official Theory Test for Cars and Motorcyclists (1998-99 edition)	ISBN 0 11 552017 1	....	£11.99
The Driving Manual	ISBN 0 11 551782 0	....	£12.99
The Motorcycling Manual	ISBN 0 11 551781 2	....	£9.99
Test Yourself Papers for the Driving Theory Test	ISBN 0 11 551984 X	....	£4.99 inc. VAT
Know Your Traffic Signs	ISBN 0 11 551612 3	....	£2.50
The Driving Test	ISBN 0 11 551778 2	....	£4.99
Driving Skills - Theory Test and Beyond CD-ROM Version II	ISBN 0 11 312062 1	....	£24.95 inc. VAT
Making A Pass (Video)	ISBN 0 11 551877 0	....	£14.99

PLEASE COMPLETE IN BLOCK CAPITALS

Name...

Address ....

....

.... Postcode........................... 984

☐ I enclose a cheque for £.................... payable to: *'The Stationery Office'*

☐ Please charge to my account with The Stationery Office: Account no:

....

☐ Please debit my Access/Visa/Amex/Connect Acc No.

Signature.. Expiry date ....

☐ Please tick if you do not wish to receive further
details on titles from The Stationery Office.
*Prices are correct at time of going to
press but may be subject to change
without notice. A full listing of terms
and conditions of sale can be obtained
on request from The Stationery Office
Publications Centre, 51 Nine Elms Lane,
London SW8 5DR.*

The Stationery Office

DS
DA
DRIVING
STANDARDS
AGENCY
'Safe driving for life'

Printed in The United Kingdom for The Stationery Office J0042948 04/98 C100 63789